MW00456250

NIGHT

ENNIO MOLTEDO

Translated from Spanish by
Marguerite Feitlowitz

WORLD POETRY BOOKS

Night by Ennio Moltedo
Copyright © The Estate of Ennio Moltedo, 2022
Published with the permission of Carla Renata Moltedo Morales.
English translation and Introduction copyright © Marguerite Feitlowitz, 2022

Originally published as *La Noche* by Ediciones Altazor (Valparaíso, 1999)

First Edition, First Printing, 2022
ISBN 978-0-9992613-6-1

World Poetry Books
New York, NY / Storrs, CT
www.worldpoetrybooks.com

Distributed by SPD/Small Press Distribution
Berkeley, CA
www.spdbooks.org

Library of Congress Control Number: 2022945856

Cover Art: Nemesio Antúnez (1918–1993), "Observatorio Nocturno," 1983
(Rome), aquatint etching (IV/XV), 69.5 x 49.6 cm. © 2022 Artists Rights
Society (ARS), New York / CREAIMAGEN, Santiago

Typesetting by Don't Look Now
Cover design by Andrew Bourne
Printed in Lithuania by KOPA

World Poetry Books is committed to publishing exceptional translations of
poetry from a broad range of languages and traditions, bringing the work of
modern masters, emerging voices, and pioneering innovators from around the
world to English-language readers in affordable trade editions. Founded in
2017, World Poetry Books is a 501(c)(3) nonprofit and charitable organization
based in New York City and affiliated with the Humanities Institute and the
Translation Program at the University of Connecticut (Storrs).

TABLE OF CONTENTS

THE HOLLOW PILLARS OF THE LAW: ENNIO MOLTEDO'S CHILEAN NIGHT

I arrived in Santiago de Chile on a blisteringly hot Sunday afternoon in early December 2016, too travel weary to go exploring. Of course, I set out anyway, unprepared for the surprising detour ahead. Wandering through Lastarria—an artsy and bustling old urban village—I turned into a little square and found myself opposite the elegantly arranged display windows of a spacious bookstore: Librería Ulises. Before long, my arms were full of recently published books I intended to buy. And then, over my shoulder, came a booming voice: "*Basta con la narrative argentina!! Este es el país de poetas!*" (Enough with the Argentine novels. This is the land of poets!) The voice came from a surprisingly delicate-looking man—Jorge Rosemary, bookseller, poet, publisher—who sat me down and for the next two hours brought me book upon book of Chilean poetry. My reaction to Ennio Moltedo was immediate and physical: it felt like the lines were passing right through me. That I am now translating Moltedo's body of work is an ongoing gift from Jorge.

Revered in Chile among readers and critics of twentieth-century Spanish-language poetry, Moltedo (1931–2012) has been compared with C.P. Cavafy for his allegiance to a city at once mythic and mundane; with René Char for the inventiveness of his political poems; with Umberto Saba for his mastery of extreme concision. For Raúl Zurita, who was arrested on the day of the 1973 coup (September 11) and imprisoned with hundreds of others in the hold of a ship,

Moltedo is "one of the finest, greatest, most curious and honorable poets of Chile. If he is not better known, it is because poetry far exceeds the times of our human lives."[1]

For poet Juan Cameron, a Chilean contemporary of Zurita and Moltedo, "Moltedo is an indispensable poet ... Nothing escapes his mordant eye, neither the exile nor he who exiles, neither the one who returns nor the one who stayed, neither the scribbler, nor the reader, nor the ignorant citizen. All share in the same poverty ... With his death, we've lost the best of our Generation of '50, of our *porteña* poetry."[2] Scholar Cristián Warnken, who edited an important collection of Moltedo's works, wrote, "Moltedo is one of the great poets ... yet to be rediscovered and re-read ... I am certain that starting now, and in years and decades to come, he will be a reference point for our young people. Not only a poetic [standard] but a moral one. There is a profound coherence between his ethics and his poetics."[3]

The author of eight collections of poems, several books of chronicles, including one about Neruda, with whom he co-translated an anthology of Romanian poetry,[4] Moltedo appears in English for the first time with *Night* [*La Noche*], a collection of 113 prose poems written during and in response to the Pinochet regime. Conscious of the way politics can leach the poetry from the act of writing poems, Moltedo let the book gestate for a number of years, not publishing it until 1999. (In fact, while Moltedo never stopped writing, he didn't publish any poems from the late 1980s until 1999; his poems had taken a dangerously political turn, which he thought best to keep private.) There is a sharpness, an "edge" in *La Noche* that marks it as a major point of inflection in Moltedo's oeuvre. These small texts range from lyric to mini-drama to what Moltedo called "micro-fiction," some being all three at once. Chilean critics, including Cameron, consider *La Noche* "Moltedo's greatest work."[5]

After his first book was published, Moltedo decided he would never again write according to externally determined meter; he delineated everything he'd written thus far and from then on only wrote poems in prose. He sought a deeper, more organic and subtle music, whose sonorities would liberate the shape of sentences, the energy of images, and produce a prosody that compels rhetorical power. Details recur in a play of quotidian familiarity, political menace, and the uncanny. He explains nothing: rather he renders, frames, and layers images in ways that both propel and challenge narrative.

Moltedo's lines are always plain in terms of diction, a trait that only heightens their mystery, lyricism, and political force. His rage is exquisitely controlled in a tight syntax and in images that appear surreal but are grounded in material fact. From the present collection, here is poem 12 in its entirety: "They have sent me to the bottom of the sea. Without oxygen, of course. In street clothes, with blue envelope in hand." The clarity of the image is at once unsettling and persuasive; the rhythm is tidal, lending a documentary quality to what's being said. (The Pinochet regime did indeed throw political prisoners into the sea.) The blue envelope alludes to the termination notice workers receive when fired—the poet had himself received such an envelope during a political shake-up at the University of Valparaíso Press, where he had long served as Director.

In one of his final interviews, carried out with the Chilean journalist and scholar Montserrat Madariaga-Caro, Moltedo spoke of strolling with a friend in the gardens of the Federico Santa María Technical University in Valparaíso, where he happened upon a large cube constructed as an architectonic homage to engineering. He drew close, knocked on the surface, and found, to his surprise, that it was hollow. This gave him an idea. He asked a friend to accompany him to the National Congress; you're my witness, he called out, then strode up the grand steps that are flanked by two enormous, imposing columns. Rapping on them with his knuckles, he found that they too were hollow. The pillars of the law supported nothing.[6]

And the scales of justice? What did they support? The licit or illicit, due process or its mere appearance? Moltedo often noted that during Pinochet's dictatorship, Parliament was shuttered but the judiciary still functioned—as an arm of the military regime. Legal terminology abounds in Moltedo's poems, and usually leads us into realms where rationality and order are facades for brutality and maniacal drive.

A native of Valparaíso, Moltedo is a poet of the sea, and his connection to ancient Mediterranean poets is manifest in his poems. A fluent reader of Latin and Italian, he was steeped in Martial, Horace, and Catullus, and in Dante (*La Noche* can be considered Moltedo's *Inferno*). He was obsessed with grammar, and all his life he kept notebooks in which he glossed grammatical rules and exceptions. His contemporary reading was at once cosmopolitan and philosophically focused; his notebooks are full of quotes from and reflections on Kafka, Camus, Cavafy, Jünger, Moravia, MacLeish, and Pessoa. Architecture and visual art were essential interests, and he drew, painted, and made collages. For over thirty years, he lived in an apartment complex designed by Le Corbusier (Las Siete Hermanas, or The Seven Sisters) in Viña del Mar.

The son of Italian immigrants, he was strongly attached to the Italian community of Valparaíso and adjacent Viña del Mar.

He staunchly refused to relocate to Santiago, Chile's capital and seat of the cultural establishment. Moltedo preferred his daily strolls along the streets of his port cities and his tight-knit circle of local writers and artists. Suspicious of any centralized power structure (especially that of Pinochet), and fiercely loyal to the values of local particulars, he writes in a late poem, "Through these streets, without leaving the city, I have followed you to the end of the world . . . never again will we meet, in this small city, at so many of the world's places."[1] Far from being sentimental or misty-eyed, Moltedo plumbs the mystery of his home port—urban enough for the never-to-be-repeated encounter or sighting, small enough to be paradoxically infinite.

Written during the decades of a military dictatorship that extended from Atacama, the world's driest desert, to the frozen expanse of Antarctica, *Night* also illuminates our engulfing political moment of brutal corruption and cruel politics, here in the US and abroad. In the face of these enemies, Moltedo wields not merely well-aimed fury, but also dead-on humor, city smarts, nonstop invention, and dialogue with centuries of world poetry. Moltedo's poems stop us in our tracks, but ultimately keep us moving—toward the light of laboring for a better future. The concept of *toward* is quintessential Moltedo. Poetry, he often said, proposes a new reality. It doesn't get there, but it continually marks the approach.

—*Marguerite Feitlowitz, September 2022*

NOTES

1 Francisco Mouat, "Ennio Moltedo," Radio ADN, article posted online February 16, 2017.

2 Juan Cameron, "Sobre Ennio Moltedo (1931–2012)," Santiago, Chile: MovingArt, published online, shortly after the poet's death, which occurred on August 14, 2012. Cameron has written extensively on Moltedo and regularly takes part in related interviews, round tables, book presentations, and so on. He was forced into exile by the dictatorship.

3 "Editorial UV presentó *Regreso al mar* de Ennio Moltedo," Notícias Universidad de Valparaíso, published online April 8, 2015. In 2005, Ediciones del Chivato published *Ennio Moltedo: Obra Poética* (the complete works to that date); *Regreso al mar* (2015) includes a generous selection from Moltedo's final book, *Las cosas nuevas*.

4 *44 poetas rumanos* [44 Romanian Poets] (Buenos Aires: Editorial Losada, 1967).

5 Cameron, op. cit.

6 "Entrevista inédita a Ennio Moltedo por Montserrat Madariaga," included in Ennio Moltedo, *Regreso al mar: antología poética,* introduction by Cristián Warnken. (Valparaíso, Chile: Editorial UV de la Universidad de Valparaíso, 2015), 245–46.

7 Excerpt from poem 32, collected in Ennio Moltedo, *Las cosas nuevas* (Viña del Mar, Chile: Ediciones Altazor, 2011), 56. My translation of this book is in progress.

NIGHT

1

At what time must the birds lined up in gardens, trees, and cages sing?

Look to the law.

2

Let's appoint the village madman. Chief Justice on the Court of Appeals, with a vote and veto and seat at the table, a sane example to the debating powers-that-be and the people who in their hours of contemplation rest in chairs set out on the sidewalk, when twilight bloodies the screen with scrolls and pictures to make us believe that, of course, here it is, the disgusting fleshy finale.

Let's appoint the village madman.

3

We'll go around the world. Walking. Just for the exercise.
As preparation. For one reason or another. Because the New
Year. Because no one can take us seriously. Just for show.
But a real show.

Tiring, for sure. Some will die and others crawl. But while
the world obsesses over absolute kingdoms, we are walking,
always walking, disinterested, to our own beat. If you lose
the beat, as everyone knows and repeats, you can never win.
Come in to see us. We're totally starched and ironed. Eyes
on the horizon. Swallowing wind, clouds, elastic borders.
Always staring, and clocking in.

The same mold. The same handiwork. Without saying a
word—that's forbidden—without hearing a single word,
having no destination, cursing birth itself, heading for the
scrim of another world.

Men walking to where men don't exist.

4

Birthdays, celebrations. I died when it was time for high
school. Since then we've seen only exhumations and the on-
going examinations—legal and illegal, underwater or lit by
the moon—so today I'm asking for a little peace, a natural
interval in which to behold the meager imagination de-
ployed in observances for the dead.

Landscapes, communal feasts, and faces immortalized in
bank calendars; traveling families and sports teams beam-
ing for the comic camera; academics and diplomats holding
a forum in the Republic of Cunaní.

But what, dear God, do you say if what matters most is the
photo.

Never forget the photo.

5

Enough huffing and puffing to show you can blow away storm clouds. Thank you; but we're tired of the spectacle with its endless supply of birds and so much hopping in and out of pockets.

Enough already with your tales of personal miracles and unprecedented surprises (as old as the hills) given that no one can see through the window or the cowl. Stop, please, if just for a moment, tastelessly bragging about the group's competence which consists, in sum, of turning flesh into newsprint.

So as not to annoy, so as to clear the sky and earth of so much progress and to restore the enigma of history, I recommend that the highest and next highest powers—well, all the powers—legislate one more step back toward night: reinstate slavery. We will return to strip the perpetual present of so much wonder.

6

Dear friends: Farewell. Death comes between us. Leaving its trademark everywhere, on the loose at all hours, observing no holidays or holy days. Happily entertained.

You abided by the instructions and after the erasures and revisions you climbed on the tables to clap for the recount. Consequences even today. Until tomorrow. Until never again.

7

Definitive sentences do not appear in these pages unless they were previously published in the newspaper of record—as the law decrees and horizons vanish.

8

Lovely performance of The Moors Overture from '36
with the uniformed—yes uniformed—trumpeters in the
balconies of the church and, below, in the street, the open-
mouthed populace and powers-that-be. From a gate in the
tower a solo machine gun marks the beat with regular
blasts and, now that it's used far less than before, it
inspires old yearnings for battle, enchanting the whole
Sunday mob of children, parents, and balloons.

Isn't there one damn soul around here who understands the
meaning of all this?

9

An excess of music entangles the hair and birds soften the heart. What do we get from flying in another language. Let's get out of here. It's a fantasy to think, like everyone else, that the parade will disappear, swallowed up by the fiery horizon.

Back from the bar crawl. Here they are, all out of control. Hollering, bursting into the house.

Mama, they signed up for the army!

It's the holidays, the movie house is full, the promenade overflows.

A few are leaning against telephone poles.

Already going bald, young men bang on their drums. Eyebrows arch above violins. Impossible to hold back tears. The birds refuse to fly; they perch, seated, as attentive as if they were in class. It's an illusion to think they sleep in trees; that they escape out the window; that they peck at the air; that velocity is gained with the feet drawn up; or that they are free.

Binoculars, mama!

10

If you put your ear to the naked earth, you will precisely
hear the murderers' names.

11

Can we go on like this? Wherever one goes, on a walk, to
work, to the desert, to the seashore, a hollow, a shelter,
anyplace in the shade, there's a message, a sign at the foot
of the column, in official gardens, among trees, even in
ponds and underwater currents, in the tunnel, yes, under
the bridge, in the office of the district attorney, by all the
evidence, from every one of our pores, we are birthing the
half-dressed dead.

12

They have sent me to the bottom of the sea. Without oxygen, of course. In street clothes, with blue envelope in hand.

13

Payment is due.

Who am I to extend credit in the middle of the musical avenue?

Payment is due, cash down on the counter or onscreen—you're free to count your bills or hit enter—but payment is being drawn on the earth, by the riot of flowers and lawns rolled out by the mile, as though it were all a gift of nature, born of a point in space, growing and stretching until it reaches us (how is it possible to conceive of something so beautiful?)

14

Advancing and retreating in a strange movement through the fog, the sea was giving us clues, and then erasing them. Appearing in the fabric of the horizon were rents of unsuspected clarity and shifting shadows, small rips at first, then blots that became forms: caves, animals, constructions hanging by a thread over the water where words and messages and fears from another world could only be read and repeated by the waves.

Then the earth pitched down in front of us, reaching for the coast which—along with your heart—kept absolute silence.

15

"*Noche*, from the Latin *nox*, from the Greek *nyntos*, descended in turn from the Sanskrit *nakta*.

In German one says *nacht*; in English, *night*, in Portuguese, *noite*; in French, *nuit*, in Catalan, *nit*, in Walloon, *nute*." In Chile, night is eternal.

16

For political reasons the authorities banished the poet.
Now an old man, he was given to know that if he showed
signs of repentance he would be allowed to return to the
fatherland.

Never, replied Dante.

For centuries Florence has solicited Ravenna for the re-
turn of the poet's remains and that city has always replied:
Never.

Never will we be capable of replying never.

17

We are the ones most capable of marching together, in uni-
son and harmony, from north to south, on the dirty road
flanked with flags, day and night, rain or shine, eyes sur-
prised by the satellite, by the cable to the moon, the wagon
of fire and the angels in their chalice of night and crystal.

You march, we march, just to leave and return, rounding
the corner, going back home by our regular bus, hun-
gry for lunch after the long white march; but the parade
is supposed to go on forever with the martial music of
death—"eternally will I mourn you"—no looking back, no
going back until we get to the edge and fall into the frozen
summit of the southern mirrors: once again the iceberg.

18

Anarchist-nihilist-revolutionist—many names but only one
father for this son who returns on a bicycle, old and naked,
a display ad hanging down his back.

19

Lucilio, after so much talk and so much verse dedicated to pretty girls you fall into the arms of a comical old lady. No one is criticizing. On the contrary, you'll learn more than you ever believed you taught.

By now you'll have realized that the silence of your young friends was only their submission to the impossibility of speech in the realm of mystery.

But now, in these old arms you'll have noted that you never stop thinking or being surprised and soon you'll recognize that here lies poetry, eternally ripe.

20

And who will take charge?

The one to take charge must doubtless be he who controls the atmosphere, the passage of years, who knows who's who in the customs and culture and closely held origins of the Service, and who comprehends, at a glance, the nature of the problem, the run-of-the-mill statue across the leafy park, the climb up the stairs, the meditative rest on the way down, and above all: that once installed on high, he be able to see himself as just like the others who go up and down; *porter* will be his elevated position.

21

Once you've been thrown out, and good riddance, you will never return to your hearth. But now you're old, invisible and inconceivable, so you turn back, set off on the road toward the place that gave you comfort: the country you called home.

But the country you called home has disappeared.

22

Well-dressed deplorables, posing face-front, in profile, gaz-
ing down, penciled and polished, casually perfect amid the
lights and squalor—how much longer?

Close-shaven masks and gold chokers, neckties securely
pinned down, a picture-ad for larded respectability, glass in
hand or triumphant aspergillum—how much longer?

The living dead brilliantly girded for power—on the escala-
tor going up—lights, camera, fanfare—how much longer?

To be continued...

23

No problem. Plowing end to end. Slitting the country end to end.

Back and forth. One furrow next to another, like bleachers in the stadium, as seen from the air, their traces sinking, ever deeper, night and day.

Until they appear. Until we hear their screaming.

We're here! My darling, here!

24

The general heart doesn't beat. Though it exists.

What we can call—in sentimental moments—the collective heart is not the sum total of individual hearts. The general heart is a unique artifact and whoever finds it can consider himself dead.

25

The important thing is that the guilty, as well as sympathizers, including assistants, be able to have Christmas with kith and kin—that is to say, their loved ones—under the tree with scintillating lights.

For the rest of the citizens: an official token intended to soothe wounds and renew the strength to forget, stand fast until the next tree with the star on top and scintillating lights.

26

The Champ—of some national competition—goes around telling how he single-handedly defeated half the world—though vulnerable, they were young and valiant—flying at low altitudes with exquisite precision, constantly transmitting, with ruses and maneuvers that were perfectly legal, and ideas, velocities, and verbal weapons that have never been revealed, which is why he's never received any saintly recognition, nothing but trotters and wings. Today all he can do is stand face-to-face, open his eyes wide and declare:

For the first time ever, I'm knocked out by what I see, it is (so, so, so) extraordinary—inner sigh number three—that I will offer it now to you. He turns and what do we see: the same assembly of moral defectives, seated in a semicircle, and appearing through a curtain of steam, a new-minted male/female idiot looking back at us.

27

Polonius: What are you reading?

Hamlet: Vehicles, vehicles, vehicles.

28

O, in these parts, we often heard Caligula's whistle, shrieking sanity in the face of poetry and the madness of the moon. Oh, this world of engineers and managers, their circus of concrete and corruption, their skimming from public funds.

The train appears, pushing toward us plumes of rain; it rumbles across the bridge, past the triangular sign and the wires, and reaching the green landscape stained with milk, the train blows its whistle, lights its interior lights, changes its music in the tunnel. The train reappears, we're on our way, a new blackboard with colored chalks, a new draft composed in our head; seas and sands reappear with Camus's sun and freedom; vanished are markets and mills and whole afternoons at the farmhouse window following the train's slow progress through the mist, the hand and pencil expanding the poem, the country's juvenile composition.

O, once again Caligula's whistle is right on schedule!

29

1937, Madrid, Ridruejo, fascist poet, goes to the Republican side; not that it made his verses any better, and the same is happening here and now, 1977.

30

Constantine: I am informing you that the city has been divided. The north side will continue on with its poor neighborhoods, student walkways under the palms, shouting in the marketplace, and the mad rush of carts competing with the train that runs above the sea.

The avenue of bicameral gods points south, toward a different Paradise Valley put in place by a giant hand where concrete tower and open pit both drool with useless power from the domains of the idiot kingdom.

Constantine: Only in dreams, with a view through the triumphal arch, is it possible to once more imagine the blue hill and a cloud that floats freely across our ancient time.

31

Let us renew our relationship with the sea, announce the authorities.

As they pull down the fence. As they tear down the curtain and sack the towers of Babel and the shacks, the bins and the dumpsters, as they pull down the chicken wire and the railings and the prison huts and the barriers and clear away the stinking piles of leaking bags and barrels and the stains from battalions of bugs—cars on the beach—shining through the filth of bonfires and paper trash, nothing new to say about this gray normality that spews its nightmares in every direction and buries the sea of our dreams.

32

Reappearance of the devil. But is it true?

Consult, examine. Serious arguments, political and theological, will take place in the agency.

The corpse's change of color will say yes but how was agreement achieved in the heart of the capital's capital. There will be hand-wringing, eye-rolling, tugging at collars and neckties. Damn it all, someone will say, the children had to be sent to the provinces and there need to be lookouts for when it enters this city of houses and subways where the market is blue with the crusts of dried blood whose dust is found on every altar or corner where you see yourself reflected and submit to all authority and eat and greet and bow and curtsy in the hope of one day getting invited to the table of toxic feasts—damn it all!

33

I denounce him with this cup of tea, says the young man, snuffing out the porcelain by closing his eyes. I denounce them with this toast to good manners, says the industrialist from his armchair, signaling for entrances and exits, directing every detail.

The curtain is coming down—who would have imagined it after so many years of experimental theater—where, for a cup of tea and a comfy seat and slaps-on-the-back among ourselves—because, it now appears, all that art and love was just a show—despite the nights and days of remembrance and remorse—who would have imagined?

At times, it becomes necessary to soften the drama, reach for consensus and set the table with glasses and cups and gilded leaves—where did these lovely old things come from—so that in this act everything will again become clear and possible and the past will be forgotten and I, director and actor, will have no illicit present or principles or sad endings.

I remember nothing and no one and all these lights and electronics are powerless to bring any of it back.

34

Come on, if they're real criminals, there's no other word: death.

35

Pious hypocrites kowtowing to the Pope.

Remember? And after every Sunday.

Their constancy and superhuman industry get them pardons from the court with jurisdiction.

Monday is a whole different thing. Pious hypocrites tunneling through every circle of hell only to get here alive and early.

36

You can stop the charade! Different times, but man still marks his moment with word and deed. Only the horizon knows what will happen from one minute to the next—if the chain of actions will melt into gas and memory and you can all relax.

We close the curtains—undulations on the sea—and refuse all visits from outside our group. Time has changed us? No one we don't know can appear among us.

It is forbidden to trademark the wind, or the water. Who is it now who's so agreeable and smiling, offering his hand to the newly minted monster? No one must invite the beast to come share—I'm not exaggerating—our playthings.

Nor to have a seat at the table and be fêted as we open the windows wide. Its darkness must deepen. We will not allow it to fade, to befoul the space we have always seen expand, stretch freely toward the line of figures and incidents coming toward us from the sea.

37

We thought we were living, growing, but we were only dig-
ging for our eternal future.

38

In times of peril and conflict its subtlest expressions are
amplified, and its dimensions expand. We're talking about
a classical artifact of unquestionable visual-aesthetic
distinction. To this day old and young dream of its form—
spherical or ovoid—and of its polished black surface. Its
volume, autonomous and hermetic, reflects equally the light
of day and night but it holds (forcefully holds) the essen-
tial secret within.

And yet one barely thickened point on its surface is im-
possible to detect with the naked eye. It alters the center of
gravity, and when the object is rolled, its trajectory is im-
possible to predict.

Self-sufficient and compact the artifact surprises as much
for its quietude and age—measurable only in time under-
ground or in aerial seconds—as for the impression it gives
of a sudden desire to be free, which it communicates only
once; then the form disappears under sponges and soap and

it's always too late to save it. This development is represented in storms of minutiae and primitive tracings: suns and spirals confirmed with rays and beams—symbols of an advanced technology!

Perhaps it's only the lights of the end of the century or suppressed fantasies; a bubble that has grown to add a little confusion and justice to the order of space, time, humankind.

39

Today, toward twilight, in our survey of the coast, of blazing Valparaíso and its darkening mirror, we tallied—and have in our hand the accounts to prove it—thirty-five thousand five hundred thirty-five vehicles streaming in from the capital. Scoundrels!

40

Anniversaries at sea are seductive. The signs persist in the prow, a border of land and tracings of the horizon after centuries of lifting anchor, when only the margins of maps and maybe a bird could imagine the seam between sky and sea and the tilt of the rose against a corner of the clouds and the sight of messages in bottles and now the whip-crack for anniversaries: the first spyglass, the shot and recoil, the flaming sail, mute syllables painted on the wind, and the replicating mirror atop, below, between the waves. Because we're drowning in anniversaries—relaunchings and rebirths—we have crossed the threshold that divided life from death and here we lie before the sea to once again navigate our own waters, the very image of unforgettable disasters.

41

Apples baking in the oven, no. Let them keep lighting up the trees, and life.

42

The great bloodhounds of information—linked in smoke and newsprint—bite or caress or muzzle according to instinct and interest in the liberty of bones.

Immortal in the fray and charmed by the golden light of cliché they reproduce the order of the day and present (to the powers that be, looking out from the balcony or boat or skateboard, "so you can know them better"), interminable lists of precepts and prescriptions relayed by chorister-conductors or the remains of friezes and casts released from the vault, which have returned a little cracked and crazed from the tyrannical twilight, with an expression of what happened here and I haven't lost anything because nothing has happened between us we're all one family—right?—all in tune, and once again they're swallowing everything and turning themselves into lynxes in the shadow of the blood-hound, the guardhouse, and the news.

43

Haven't you been dreaming of a brilliant voyage?

Why don't I blow you into the beyond, critic: through a
tube or a good stiff straw, you'd stream into the heavens,
flashing your taillights and giving off sparks.

A rocket, something new, for the future, a navigator floun-
dering with skirts in the wind but, finally, floating ink
tinting the best page for an absolute reading among the
stars, and a last farewell from those of us standing fast in
the land of humans.

44

Protect me, God, from pedagogical meaning, and let each
day surprise my sight with the breeze that blows—in no
style—past the corner.

45

Observe them. Listen to them. That's right: you can't believe a single word. It's pure disguise. They piss platitudes and shit clichés which they trade like ingots of gold and then go stealing from your grandma.

Oh! Where can we find the horizon with its arms wide open, embracing the colors rippling on the water, flowing down through the clouds, like weavings in the wind, such bursts of color—Casa Peirano—even the fish gasp out bubbles and sigh!

Observe them. Listen to them. That's right: our eminent jurists.

Mythical laws of the land and repeating refrains in the halls of power, plaques on the houses of families that gather for meals, the scales so heavily weighted we're out on the streets, flat broke, no more breath. Oh, my zócalo of clear blue sea that extends toward the nothing that slowly descends over the port and delights us with a different landscape each morning and evening.

46

This portal to the sky, washed by the wind, these peaks are more colorful, clean, and whole than any "city center" of smoke clouds, crates, and a new form of congress—piles of bones the whole length of the beach, yellowing under the sun, the architecture of some prehistoric beast.

47

It's fine that you zoom off on the clouds riding high in your saddle of smoke, singing songs in another language that the wind carries far away.

It's fine that you're thinking of poetry and of the friends in your tribe and that you all get high and write like someone performing their task in the spectacle now to be seen on every corner.

It's fine—the coffee and beers and the book under your arm and the diploma proving you completed the workshop, and the interview, and the profile of the stupid celebrity, and the odious clouds that—you say—don't adequately yield or descend—as in the videos—to climb or perch on. But who can accomplish something new and genuine if there isn't any clarity on what happened yesterday and we don't know how to read the space between ourselves and others?

48

Toga, cassock, fool's cap?

49

Good for you, Galileo. You escaped by a hair. Now, in November of 1992, you are officially vindicated.

As for our Juan, his case is just getting started: with no papers or proofs there's no possible hurry, but let's hope it doesn't take five hundred years.

50

If you are still young: Don't register, don't sign up. Don't sit waiting at desks in nauseating sinkholes, among the leavings of greasy meals and old papers flying through the dust, mindlessly repeating the same old thing.

Instead, walk out to the sunlit shore where the first frontier of the rest of the world begins and the horizon is clear, with clean answers to every young question.

51

Please, no. Not the full weight of the law.

Where do they come from, the flowers that bloom by the wayside and blossom in the constitution—and always face the same direction?

Impossible to resist the white boys' legislation. Impossible, so much weight and so much paving over. To tell you the truth, I prefer to sit back and wait for the presidential reckoning, the early and definitive iterations, all the usual music on which—they say—the very air, this time of year, depends.

I prefer a carillon concert or the same old movie shown on the clear channel of the fog:

I prefer the story of Hermes the fascist who in '39 sailed off, amid cheers and applause, to defend the peninsula, and in '45 was seen returning from the opposite side of the boat, on the arm of the enemy.

But the whole weight of the law, no, not here. The children are sleeping.

Leave something for the moment we pack the truck. For the night of bags and bundles. For our escape. But also for a weekend, in the sun, with the memory of friends. These things are not to be gambled with.

52

The navy's newspaper: pictures and news: views of the sea,
replete with bubbles, fancy formations, drills in approach
and departure, change of direction, collision, curfew,
whistle, looping the loop. Here is the log, the lectern. The
records of this armored tomb scuttle the past, the chains
of command and their respective colors, the lunges and
sidesteps—practically a tango—changes in position a bit
before not after, on the beat! *vamos!* more courage than
caution, maiden sailings and handrails above a cheap lit-
tle basin of sea.

53

Who's swallowing this mess begotten by the model?

The same unfortunates as always.

54

He started in school. Selling fruit and bread to his class-
mates. Then pencils, rubber bands, sponges.

Today, to acclaim, he is selling the country; by parts, by
zones, fertile or arid, blue above or below, and he'd sell his
mother if he still had her.

A new mother is what he needs to be sold once and for all.

55

The iguana kept silent for years but now it's licking its lips
again and pointing its tongue at those who should disap-
pear—aesthetically, I mean—at those it allows to bite into
the fruit and those who can publicly display their art if it
has been sold in compliance with the ten-point instructions
on the form.

To he who dares to opine on my behalf saying he's pro-
tecting me from the night, from the flowers of evil, from
the excess of light, and who from his post in the tower
dispenses counsel from above or below the stocks, bad for
children, bad for the country—here being the birthplace
of Vicente's "O," though good for the good of evil, do me a

favor, shut your beak. Please crow for your own private purpose, platform, or brotherhood. Please consult directly with your suck-up personnel. Please stop praying with the *sambenito* under your bed. Please lift up your skirts and stick your fears and videos up your own moral ass.

56

As long as we keep talking to exculpate the setting sun, night will always surprise us and there will be no solution for tomorrow. Tomorrow will be the eternal anniversary. Memory gets a quick burial. Isn't that what best suits us?

We must live here and tremble. What's the point of denying it when more than once we've circled the globe? Notwithstanding the music, the leaders-of-the-moment declaiming to the delight of the high-and-mighty—September, how splendid—dawn dressed up for night.

57

Write me a law, write it by hand. A law that lays down
a life sentence: to read and listen to poetry. Including
the epic, with its pre-fab prosody and caterpillar cadence:
rhymed gunshots and bared breasts to excite the listener,
and then what happens, happens.

Write me a law with a gold-tipped pencil on a table in the
burnt-out palace so I can legally—always legally—spend the
rest of my life safe and snug and laughing at all the movies.

A law, a law so we can breathe! Or at least an ordinance,
something simple and local that will let us live in some
cranny while the wind carries off—or carries in?—the
sound of guns.

58

The same ones complaining today of the cold shoulder—
what crybabies—used to applaud the lightning strike of
the law.

The same ones who partied in banks now fold their hands,
lower their eyes, and ask from another world: "Does your
honorable self, and do the family of your honorable self,
enjoy the bounties of good health?"

Such courtesy! Such composure!

59

Eternal past of the chichi present: it returns in the form
of electric shocks to what remains of our country: power
grids and grinning statistics in the precincts of war—head-
lines and smoke—and moving parts that appear with just
a touch of the finger, like packaged pudding, thanks to the
science devoted to envelopes, lids, and tubes to the void; a
similar specialty: inflated diving suits and trash bags and
private-practice surgery until the last breath of hope that
life's rhythm will be eternal, a trademarked fantasy, avail-
able on shelves and in heaps and piles of discarded old
knockoffs; family choruses of instructions and edifying
stories for children; but the terror, bottled and placed on
our path between gardens, is stronger, a preamble to war,
persistent to this day in the trembling of the chin—do you
remember the film-interview, just outside the garden, when
the connection, at nightfall...

Eternal is the past of the chichi present.

60

Dwarfs wearing suits and ties play the bailiffs in films about extraterrestrials.

61

The model comes complete, sir (and all those who want to manage the future).

Not only has it meant a triumph for vision—the colors come to life—a showcase for new functions, display windows with new names and materials, the illusion of etiquette for newborns, the newly arrived and the fallen, but, sir (and all those who clamor to show their support), the model also expresses its contradiction or quota for extermination and we—fortunately?—are meeting our goals, our numbers are growing, spinning on the rollers, spangling the sanctified paper.

Sometimes the crime, sir, seems a blessing.

62

Giving and taking. I hold out to you a certificate of good conduct and you make your confession, you whisper in my ear where they are to be found.

There will be no reports in the press and no discussion in front of the children. All quiet. What is not known does not exist. But you should know that in the future the surprise can be repeated as many times as may be necessary.

As many times as may be necessary.

63

Let's search for a bit of truth between the garbage dumps
and mechanical shovels. Among the backpacks and stroll-
ers, the puppy-face ear muffs and kitty-cat pillows, monkeys
and civilians on the warpath, and ladies running mad
around the gameboard offering their teats—amid towers of
corpses—to the king, excellent ladies distributing clothes
when decrepit nags in harness and ribbons begin the
pageant (eternal will be the pageant you gave me) among
banners and bursts of color.

I search for truth in the books discarded in the square, in
the dreams of sleeping cats and the intelligent gaze of dogs
that roam through the gardens of Congress.

64

I fell—at the last hour, when I thought I'd survived—into
the list of the dead. Among innumerable names and accu-
mulated crosses on the battlefield of your heart.

65

The crime in question is simple, the very simplest, the hearing in an empty courtroom—on a beautiful morning, on yet another anniversary, of the first periscope-eye (maritime pipeline), of the first attack, etcetera—and any entry into the record (what's the point) will be completely and forever annulled, therefore, as was heard in the sunlit courtroom empty of people and memories, let us adjourn to celebrate the living past paid for by the dead present.

Repeat this song until doing so leaves you completely indifferent.

66

One more skeleton and I'll be left talking to myself, buying bones, playing the flute, playing the drums, with bones, pointing the way to fields, plantations, and nurseries, until the day of the harvest and the great exportation of stems and bones.

67

Fearless from behind the window. From a distance. Fearless on the telephone. During interviews. Trusting in divine providence and with faith in abiding institutions, with degrees and titles engraved on plaques of bronze or copper, rate charts written in pencil with eraser—along with sketches of castles and cats—heedful of the headlines of the hour, messages that might be crossed or eternal, and in this way always keep going, keep driving, always on display, daring and dashing.

Even asleep determined to get ahead and even on holiday makes sure the business keeps running—refusing to miss out on Miami—aggressively attends the private wedding rehearsal, or dance party, or military promotion, and, suddenly, the pledge or promise or announcement is read, the photo taken from the left—or is everyone on the right, these days?—appearing on page one and implanted in the wall of power.

68

All along the coast we gaze, through a hollow, at the sea.

A patch of blue. A sign of negligence.

There's centralized authority over taxes and fumes, and smiles and assistance are disallowed and there are instructions (read them carefully) for filling gaps and there will always be one more prohibition, so there are more laws, laws, laws: blindfolding the country.

69

I've been reading you in your new specialty and now I have proof that time misleads and mellows and loosens its grip; your ideas come forth new and fresh, inspired by the sea and the green earth, even shining with a little love.

And I believe you, I think you're honest, I have proof that you've meditated long enough for this time of agreements, pacts, oblivion, and readjustments.

70

Its power is grotesque. Always and everywhere, in the least appropriate places, it's the constant refrain: US$.

Price-fixed morality.

71

Impossible, K, to enter the castle. The castle has no name, no owner, and is always empty. Even so, we must strive for the sky: realm of the scintillating promise: Freedom.

72

To all you solemn clowns, you exhibitionists of papal
bulls and rulings from the bishops, of military orders and
epaulets, of teas in high places, to all you crusaders and
beribboned fanatics, to all of you who say you hate all this
and are only helping the nation to get ahead: I raise my
middle finger.

To the new political-poetical-danceable vogue that any-
where and everywhere opens its mouth and recites, cravenly
swaying to the beat—what a show—defiler of art and the
family—what a scene—you striving midgets, making your
websites and platforms, building functions and widgets,
dragging forth books, inscriptions, and collections, all re-
fried for your visual and social consumption.

73

When death was out grazing you were all happy. You were
all happy when death lay in wait in the squares and roads
and walkways. You were all happy—raising a glass, lift-
ing your face to the sun—each time the tally showed one
enemy more, one enemy less. Now, where do things stand?
You must wait, wait for dates and proceedings, you scour
the news, you parse your recollections, you're alert to
sounds and names, peering from your caged-in balconies
like protected birds listening for footsteps, for a signal,
night, a symbol, the last hour striking: "Cibo per vivere."

74

Any middling mind could see that under these laws of
night we would fail to reach contentment.

75

To demonstrate valor and bring prestige back from the
dead, they kill. For the sake of life—unified, sanctified life,
devoted to all that is holy.

In your name, in the name of women and children, order,
the law, the family, so that all will go well as the young
take their first—so important—steps, and then go out into
the world, as much for self-improvement as for excursions
to the south, to the islands; so that no one will be de-
prived, so that everyone will be independent and private in
times of crisis and able, for example, to unload obligations
without restrictions or red tape, longings or old regrets; so
that everyone can take advantage of these years, these good
times, and the opportunity—at low cost—to enjoy these
festival days and the wide open market, technology and
investment, and have the last word, and press lawsuits until
the end of the world, etcetera.

(Further reporting prohibited, repeat the first paragraph,
Law of Internal State Security.)

76

She thinks she's protecting herself under the dome, banishing the very rays that serve to illuminate the streams and flowers—plastic frost—through which a son of the soil turned rapper is making his way. He's going to the mill house—car, pool, antennas—to see his neighbor, the mill wife, stretched out, inflated, on a floating raft, basking in the sun, after greasing the machines and getting the "overalls"—her workers—to work.

It's easy to observe these changes from a distance, efforts once devoted to the fields now fire up machines: and here's the flowering: the kingdom of screens in the realm of gods spinning in their own spaces, protected from the songs and stories of the earth.

77

The declaration was deemed, once again, to have
breached the heights of stupidity. Impossible to gauge the
dimensions.

Have you all forgotten this? Why aren't you marching
through the night, celebrating, seizing the spoils from your
achievement, paying each other off. Hasn't the Organization
taken notice, making you part of nocturnal history? From
here, from the port, flushed out into the world.

78

Simple: either you clear a path to fight on the front lines or
you go down to the catacombs. What a waste of jumping
then standing still for the snapshot, toothy as skele-
tons gathered round the piano, and of the musical scale
stretched with cable and guitar to the infinite stars.

Below, on the floor, light in the crannies, through num-
bered cells we can enter and exit the sites of sacrifice,
and share our thoughts with bones like our own, with
remains—abandoned like ourselves—on the forces that un-
live us until we die.

79

And the group photograph—a cliché of itself—showing the
finger on the hand and the hand on the glass and the glass
colored by the spotlights on thousands of participants, voy-
eurs peeping at themselves, depicted as firm and funereal,
straight on, in a semicircle, eternally identical, all lined
up—one more, please—while the focus sweeps across time,
travels the paths of art-industry-commerce, descends evenly,
and captures them all.

80

Homage to the dead: Virgil, dressed always in black, is
present in the stadium, a stress note in the sea of white
tunics.

81

Ideal investment: Forget, forgive, entomb.

82

Instead of so much eye-rolling and moralistic pouting
today, a time of peace, why didn't you utter a single word
in times of death, dickhead?

83

Ever the iguana. Especially when you hold forth and
get tongue-tied. What's going on? So much work to put
things right while the years were transforming you—from
seraph—to sergeant.

It's true you had no choice, someone had to stand vigil for
the sake of verse—especially when upstairs they're blast-
ing music right above your bed—and put some order in
all that jive.

But how unfitting to the general mission; how unfortunate
that pants and jacket have replaced the tunic. To say noth-
ing of the shrunken neck and the nose—degenerated from
classic to postmodern—O how this aggrieves you. We could
eternally enumerate such ills, that's how we progress from
a state of virtue and good intentions to one of censure, ap-
proving poems only if they're fit to be served on a platter.

We believe we are infallible in our work, unerring unto heaven—isn't that the standard?—it's the same pit of arrogance all over again and the same game against losers and suckers. Isn't that the way you put it?

84

They can be found framed by the heavens and the many-colored clouds, the heroes with name and rank, dates and decorations. And in some unknown place: the actors disappeared from their own theater.

85

Why are you going to see the old man?

It's a lie that he fought in the war and returned in the famous submarine. You know very well it's all blather and bullshit. Only one tub around here: the dumpster on the highest hill of Valparaíso.

"Adiós, Führer." It's true that the old man liked to show off with his binoculars and collections of tin flags and bird-emblazoned gothic beer steins—these carry a lot of weight for us—and photographs of white ladies forever floating like seafoam—in our memory—in theaters and baths full of vapors, even though we know they're no longer there, that they've flown away and are now part of these same clouds of our history that we had to repeat.

Why are you going to see the old man?

86

Someone, perhaps on another page, will say, what happened
to the light, to the orange sphere suspended in a play of
verticals high on an urban hill—the one that pirates hacked
to pieces and buried in the dirt—and to you, ever on the
shore, fingers tangled on the old keyboard, and above, the
invisible hulking wind grabbing leaves and birds.

Someone will say, it's time to return to the space where
drops hung suspended as the sun passed, in the empty blue.

I believe in death, in death's eternal pulse, and I believe our
moment will come again when the sea regains its color and
the sphere lights up, emblazons the hilltop, and celebrates
the dignity—this time—of the sick at heart.

87

Your Majesty (see: flag of the Kingdom of Sweden): thanks to your shelter thousands of Chileans can yet sleep, the sleep of the living.

88

We must pick a distant place and go. Or are we staying here, for business as usual, among clowns—midgets on stilts—while everyone else piles into taverns, or heads for the beach?

We must keep marching around the dry water tank, stretch, haul ourselves up, fold half our body over the edge, so we can peer down at the progress of the satisfied, deserving, exemplary column of ants arriving at their winter barrack (abandon all hope of protection at the door) where they will torture the cicada.

We must pick a distant place and go. Where there won't be armies, wannabes, or robbers guarding the gates, no magazines devoted to banking, or glittering old women with their unctuous preening, superimposed on the night. We need to pick a distant place and go. To stifle the drums and the blows that can yet be stifled.

89

Spring is delayed, nowhere to be seen. We search for her, peering into the wind that courses between the trees in the plaza.

Today in the port the season shines. Flowers and wings cover the coconut palms, and bright-breasted parrots swoop down and flutter at the ceremonial height of the Congress.

90

The night was like day: moon. The moon was like a sun: night. Impossible to know the time, the place, the reasons between so much light and shadow.

I woke not knowing where. I had to count on my fingers. I had to call on the phone. Use my tongue.

They all lie: the director, the accused, the doctor.

They all lie, each with his pre-arranged face, and counsel for the defense explains that it's a matter of opinion, and that back-and-forth is how the flag blows.

91

How he rears up, how he rises now in defense, the sad
young man of the right, with no apparent motive, no ra-
tional reason, if we consider that twenty years ago he was
cosseted, protected by the angel of bullets and ballots.

92

And what shall we do with all the love accumulated in dis-
tant countries?

Return the ashes.

93

Curfew prowls through the night, killing. So you can sleep.
So you'll wake up refreshed, so routine and security can
proceed unmolested, without the escape of a single word.

Moon stays silent—what else can you expect from that
skeleton!—repeating the only inaction it knows: shine and
fade.

The knock at the door. Despite the anonymous leaflet and
the new items proffered by the importer—manuals, flares,
cameras—always this hope that midnight will bring its
reward.

The ringing of the bell, the echo of truncheons, protect
as never before our peace on earth, keep safe the dove of
oblivion, guard the silent start of the aerial processions
and underground caravans of death.

94

A commission, an investigation, a trial, and the whole cabal to get back to the beginning and tell it all over again: the open-mouthed innocents in the front row have just arrived for the show and the same drama can be repeated. No danger to speak of: they don't know the plot, we're the professors, in this way a new generation gets a taste and swallows it down: a commission, an investigation, a trial.

95

Sea view. At sunset. Luckily deserted. Up here: signals and shouting and spinning round. Hands high.

Instant reply. Spring-loaded trigger. More signals and shouting: drop down stay prone crawl forward one, two, three shovel-lengths of sand, kissing-close to the dock, a sudden command and this time we're penalized for non-presentation of the enemy—the enemy is eternal and invented according to our needs—while the sun goes down without any resistance and bathes in the sea, as though nothing else was happening.

96

Celebration. At the far edge of the sea the horizon extends
hospitality. They set out, skipping through the water,
ridiculous in the vastness, heading for the boat, on the
way to their private landscape, the country house, the blue
ranch, *Cheers! Chin-chin!* lunch on the waves, at table until
evening tea.

Black and white are the fancy lights spanning the prome-
nade by the sea that is pulling away from the shoreline, to
escape from so much clamor and clinking and "all this is
mine forever."

97

And so, by a simple act on paper—mental magic—all
crimes committed before March 11 disappear.

Are they repentant? They're satisfied and with a draft of
mandrake they'd do it again considering the results. Mar-
velous to remember that we can all disappear without fuss
or farewells. Though it's disconcerting to hear that nothing
of the kind can ever be repeated, that for us it will never
be possible and that it was all just a puff of smoke, a ticket
out, a necessary point of sale in honor of our honor.

98

I'm observing myself. I have one eye too many. Although at first it doesn't seem so. If only everything obeyed the laws of mental labor, of disciplined effort. But no. I am guilty, profoundly guilty, of idle reading, with no goal or utility, a simple pastime, among dames and pirates and the undesirable inhabitants of dark corners, in jungles full of bellicose pygmies and shaven goddesses and, with my good remaining eye, guilty of careful reading: Wise Wind and Black Wind, dragons of the night, pillagers and villagers up in arms and, most important of all, in the siren call of books: life itself, buried truth, enigmatic justice and the unending exploration of the chasms and dangers that surge up without warning from the crypts of the sea.

Facing the bright sea illuminated by the mirror I affirm that I have, definitively, lost an eye that was truly one too many and, therefore, am unable to appreciate that which is ill seen: upright vision.

99

In order to delimit the territory, more mine than yours,
to secretly maneuver and make money they spread a steel
mesh the whole length of the port where, though it's hard
to believe, they're installing and clearing away mirrors.

It's imperative to see everything that moves.

Why be surprised if when you touch the sea, without a
guide, examine a fish, for no particular reason, or worse yet,
do nothing against the wind, that the guards come after
you for invasion of eminent domain—the immaculate hori-
zon that mustn't be seen on a whim or a simple stroll.

100

To each their sentimental backdrop. The young woman
keeps her cracked doll and the young man his trophies and
there's someone who keeps their attack knife—vanities of
the spirit—in a display case or on a desk along with utility
bills and family photos.

Disparities, unforgettable aftertastes caressed by time.

101

Nearly transparent, only just arrived, he climbs up on the pedestal and belts out his song. But who is it, man or bird? We'll find out in the next chapter.

102

Someone is lying: day and night. I don't know how we got to this page when sparklers and balloons, released by some magnetic force, are flying all over the plaza.

Manna: everyone eating his neighbor. Nasty to the marrow. Look at the signs: arrows affixed to balconies and windows and once again the boor in charge talking about something new: business.

103

This city, Catalina, cannot follow you. The city is sinking as buildings rise.

The city is disappearing in the current art of construction —authorities and architects fawn on the moneybags— revealed as its opposite in the subterranean night. Naturally suns nailed to a false-ceiling-horizon or to a corner wall revolve without rest.

Final disaster for this city of shadows where windows gaze inward, and gates are painted with the dead and luminous sea.

104

At this price and, what's more, in the dead of winter, after forty-four years of accounting—never seen it raining, like it is today, never—don't give me health at the price fixed by your house of ill repute. Life? Death, of course, Mr. Minister of Health.

105

Yes, of course: in the end, we found the guilty ones, aliens overrunning the route.

We were not alone: we had to be tough.

It's true: we were outnumbered. But for quality we hold the record. Which is why we will never lose first place when it comes to terror.

It's good to appear peaceful. As justification for the paragon of modern crime. There's no trace of the past, or anything like "observe the laws of force."

Let the misinformed geezers have their rest and the new generation go out on attack!

Although it's true, absolutely true, that since time immemorial those laws gave us total power and this star has never lost its cushion of sky and purity and the Western, Christian breath of our guardian angels, who got bloodied each time it was in our interest.

Which is why we're still in first place when it comes to being free and up-to-date. And we can never go back or repent or show our face because we follow orders and keep secrets.

Yes, there is something visible in the invisible.

106

Law, power, and terror align today against liberty, laughter, and the unprotected.

107

Once upon a time there was a crystal fish that navigated the waters of the estuary, all day long swimming round and round, up and down, no one taking note.

But don't believe everything people say. There were those who applauded the fish and the repression—how else could it be—and at the same time silently prayed that with each day the latter would become softer and softer.

108

The dead will not come back. There will be no return on their spirit. Why even talk about assets and socially conscious investments? Who are we to talk or write about such things?

The holdovers—the living—will for all time frolic with their families and flunkies, build their towers and spread their view over waters and continents.

The fatherland—Almighty Green: next of kin unknown.

109

Let us never again suffer an eclipse.

The tension in the sky and the silence of the birds left us swamped in the echoes of a circular vastness. Today, they're saying the light has returned; but nothing has changed and a cluster of shadows keeps talking and talking, wheezing and snoring—like the dead—not letting anyone breathe.

Surging up through the streaming pennants of the sun are figures that evoke the allure of power and crime.

110

Authority: absurdity: they're watching the moon. The
eclipse of the moon.

Authorities can foil the perversities. Unless they're chained.
Weighed down. Selected for mutually agreed-upon goals.
Everyone knows: they accepted unacceptable conditions.
This cannot be the same moon we had as children. It's
just that it's night, the path is full of shadows and we can
believe anything: stupidities, half-baked—and served on a
platter on page one—to attract all the flies. There's no doubt
that love is a many-splendored thing (the song or the fa-
therland?). Especially if it blunts the enemy's intelligence.

So, reporters and recorders, all together: "What are you
feeling?"

111

You are not my property. But, for a moment, I can bring elements together, put my desires in motion. As the curtain comes down and covers the landscape, beyond the road and avenue, you will occupy the place where figures and actions rise as one between cloud and horizon, as is happening this very instant with the line of birds hewing close to the moving train. They're flying low over the surface of the water toward the exact expression of speed that can be read against the twilight's lofty eye as it blinks for the last time, until morning.

112

True or false? What's important is whether the cleansing process was done inside or outside the garden. And the date. Here you find the particulars of public law.

Criminal or innocent? Whether surrounded by flowers or in the middle of the desert you've savored the fruits of crime and won't stop until you reach the final circle. Here you'll find justice.

113

We wait for them on the blue shore. Let them come from every corner. Rag-sellers, cure-sellers, wandering tale-tellers, ad-runners, errand-runners, the shamefaced, the abased, and etcetera.

The sea washes them naked and carries away the slime.

NOTES TO THE POEMS

POEM 4: The Republic of Cunaní (1886–1891) was located on the border between Brazil and French Guiana. Its establishment was facilitated by French geographer/journalist Paul Quartier, who visited the territory and made an arrangement with local chiefs who were hostile to Brazil. They declared the area a Republic, sent out for recruits, and received some three thousand replies. Neither France nor Brazil recognized the new Republic, each trying to assert its own claims of control. Gold was discovered there, in 1894; not long after, the two countries asked Switzerland to mediate their longstanding conflict over dominion of Cunaní. In 1897, most of the territory went to Brazil.

POEM 8: "The Moors Overture from '36" is a reference to the traditional festival performance of *Moros y Cristianos* [Moors and Christians]. Originating in sixteenth-century Spain, the musical spectacle celebrated the recapture of the vast peninsular territory occupied by Muslims (Moors) since the eighth century. In 1936, it would have been part of Franco's propaganda campaign in Chile, "Moors" standing in for a more generalized political "other."

POEM 28: The train and its whistle is an abiding trope in Chilean poetry; rail routes mostly travel on a north-south axis, spanning a great deal of this long slender country. According to Juan Andrés Figueroa, this poem harks back to Moltedo's time as a student at a boarding school in bucolic inland Villa Alemana. Trains then were often given names from antiquity, such as "Cyclops" or "Caligula."

Moltedo's adolescent memories and readings of Camus clearly over-lap in this poem.

POEM 38: The phrase "avenue of bicameral gods" refers to the bicam-eral parliamentary system consisting of the Senate and Deputies (*Diputados*).

POEM 45: Casa Peirano is a landmark building in Valparaíso, erected in 1911, one of the brilliantly colored houses on the hills overlooking the sea.

POEMS 47 & 55: Moltedo uses the word "vídeo," to refer to video cassette tapes. The book was written in the era of the VCR. The poet vastly preferred movie houses.

POEM 51: Moltedo is likely making reference to Andrea Hermes, who in 1939 left Chile as a communist and returned a fascist in 1945.

POEM 55: "Vicente's O" refers to *Altazor o el viaje en paracaídas* [Altazor, *or* a Voyage by Parachute, 1919] by the great avant-garde Chilean poet Vicente Huidobro (1893–1948); in Chile, *La Noche* was pub-lished by Ediciones Altazor.

POEM 61: The poem riffs on lines from the Chilean national anthem.

> Puro Chile, es tu cielo azulado.
> Puras brisas te cruzan también.
> Y tu campo de flores bordado
> Es la copia feliz del Edén.

(How pure, Chile, is your blue sky.
And how pure the breeze that blows across you.
Your land embroidered with flowers
Is a perfect copy of Eden.)

"Copia feliz" is a printer's term meaning "exact copy." (This term in the anthem has sometimes been translated—literally and sentimentally—as "happy-copy.") The pertinent lines in Moltedo's original come toward the end of the poem, where the presses are rolling, the papers imprinted with manipulated statistics and misleading information: "recién vamos acercándonos a los niveles y las cifras giran y crecen sobre rodillos y papel *copia-feliz*."

POEM 67: Luis Andrés Figueroa has called this poem a "portrait of Homo Chilensis Pinochetista." That the protagonist sketches "castles and cats" is doubly emblematic and contradictory: the castle denoting grandeur, the cat a denigrated version of the royal lion. In Chile, to say that something is "puro gato" is to mean that it's déclassé.

POEM 76: Moltedo uses the archaic "aldeano" and "aldeana" to refer to what I translate, respectively, as "son of the soil" and "mill wife."

POEM 86: The "orange sphere" refers to the towering kinetic sculpture by Jesús Rafael Soto. Installed in 1996 on a hill in Caracas, Venezuela, it was composed of 1,800 aluminum rods suspended from a 39-foot gantry. Its appearance and dynamism depended in great part on the viewer's vantage point and the play of light. Known as "The Utopian Sphere," and/or "The Caracas Sphere," and/or "The Orange Sphere," it immediately became a cultural icon, but, as the poem recounts, it was badly vandalized (during a time of economic distress and social upheaval), its parts strewn or buried in the dirt. It has since been reconstructed and installed in a more prominent location, where viewers have 360-degree visibility.

POEM 88: An exceptional example of Moltedo's freighted concision: "(dejad en la puerta toda esperanza de canto)." We have here a triple layering of reference. Beyond Dante's "Abandon all hope those who enter here," there is also an allusion to prison and other types of captivity, in which contexts "singing" means confessing to or accusing others of transgressions as a plea for mercy (mercy here being unavailable). Additionally, the line alludes to a military context, because "de canto," in military terms, refers to well-formed, well-trained, stalwart units, and can also be a reference to battle campaigns accompanied by music. "Torres de canto" refers to the towers atop medieval forts. My thanks go out to Luis Andrés Figueroa for alerting me to the prison and military references.

POEMS 102-103: Moltedo was enraged by so-called "urban renewal" projects that wrecked traditional neighborhoods, blighted the seaside and surrounding environment, and fueled corruption. Such projects were a hallmark of "progress," as defined by the brutal economics of the dictatorship.

TRANSLATOR'S ACKNOWLEDGMENTS

My first thanks go out to Arturo Fontaine Talavera, to whom I owe my initial visit to Chile, as a Distinguished Speaker at the 2016 Human Rights and Culture Conference sponsored by the University of Chile Law School. Poet, novelist, and scholar, Arturo answered every question he could, and when a query stumped him, always offered a contact who could help. During this first visit, bookseller Jorge Rosemary introduced me to the work of Ennio Moltedo, opening a whole new chapter in my life as a literary translator. The poet's editors and dear friends, Patricio González and Ernesto Pfeiffer, could not have been more generous with their time and guidance, especially at the beginning of this project. Montserrat Madariaga-Caro, whose own writing on Moltedo is luminous and insightful, was always happy to answer questions and chat about the fascinating city of Valparaíso. From Buenos Aires, Cristina Fraire helped decipher mysterious lines; in parsing the geometry of Moltedo's vision and constructions, her photographer's eye was invaluable. For his eagle eye, sharp ear, immersion in Chilean culture and politics, I thank my Bennington colleague and dear friend Jonathan Pitcher. With Neil Blackadder (Editor, *Another Chicago Magazine*) and an anonymous reader at *Delos*, I had a most enjoyable and fruitful back-and-forth about "small" details. In Santiago, Virgilio Rodríguez—poet, scholar, and expert on the work of his friend Moltedo—was a fount of information, encouragement, and guidance. In Valparaíso, I was enriched by the generosity, knowledge, and critical perspectives of Luis Andrés Figueroa, Claudio Leiva, and Macarena Roca.

I am deeply grateful to the National Endowment for the Arts for a Translation Fellowship that enabled me to set time aside to work on Ennio Moltedo. A Bennington College Faculty Research Grant help defray some travel costs. The poet's daughter, Carla Moltedo Morales, granted her authorization for my translations, and I am grateful for her confidence. I wish also to thank the editors of *Another Chicago Magazine, Anomaly, Asymptote, Azonal, Delos, The Nation, New Poetry in Translation*, and *World Literature Today*, who published earlier versions of selected translations.

At World Poetry Books, my thanks runneth over to Peter Constantine, Brian Sneeden, and especially to Matvei Yankelevich, who read and commented on several sets of proofs, was intensely involved in the art and design of the book, and just did everything to make this publication a pleasure.

As with every one of my books, my husband, David Anderson, read multiple drafts, never stinting on support, or holding back his penetrating questions.

To each and all, mis gracias de corazón.

ABOUT THE COVER ARTIST

Born in Santiago in 1918, Nemesio Antúnez was a prominent Chilean painter, muralist, and printmaker. At the age of seventeen, a high school award took him to Paris where he encountered the artwork of Pablo Picasso, Juan Gris, and Joan Miró. In the late 1940s, after a Fulbright-funded MA at Columbia University, he stayed in New York to work at Atelier 17 with Stanley William Hayter, known for his application of older printmaking techniques to Surrealist art. Antúnez returned to Santiago in the early 1950s and founded the influential printmaking center and school Taller 99 in 1956. Around that time he was also commissioned to paint several murals, which can still be seen in Santiago and Valparaiso, as well as mosaics inspired by the ceramics of Quinchamalí. Although the illusionistic geometry in his 1960s prints and paintings has drawn comparisons to Op Art, Antúnez remained an adherent of the Surrealism which inspired him as a young artist. His dreamlike images of crowds either rioting or submissive, barriers on the verge of the visible, twisted beds, and chairs writhing in checkerboard seas read as enigmatic allegories, both personal and political. Since his death in 1993, he is remembered as a prolific artist and pioneer printmaker, as well as an innovative educator and promoter of the arts.

Nemesio Antúnez (1918–1993), "Observatorio Nocturno," 1983 (Rome), aquatint etching (IV/XV), 69.5 x 49.6 cm. © 2022 Artists Rights Society (ARS), New York / CREAIMAGEN, Santiago

The text of *Night* is typeset in Hermann, a typeface designed by Chilean type designers Diego Aravena Silo and Salvador Rodríguez for W Type Foundry in Santiago, Chile, in 2018. Titles are set in Titular, designed by Daniel Hernández and Luciano Vergara for Latinotype, a Chilean typeface distributor founded in 2008. The cover and series design is by Andrew Bourne; the artwork is by Nemesio Antúnez. Printed and bound by KOPA in Lithuania.

WORLD POETRY BOOKS

Jean-Paul Auxeméry | *Selected Poems*
tr. Nathaniel Tarn

Maria Borio | *Transparencies*
tr. Danielle Pieratti

Jeannette L. Clariond | *Goddesses of Water*
tr. Samantha Schnee

Jacques Darras | *John Scotus Eriugena at Laon*
tr. Richard Sieburth

Olivia Elias | *Chaos, Crossing*
tr. Kareem James Abu-Zeid

Phoebe Giannisi | *Homerica*
tr. Brian Sneeden

Nakedness Is My End: Poems from the Greek Anthology
tr. Edmund Keeley

Jazra Khaleed | *The Light That Burns Us*
ed. Karen Van Dyck; tr. Peter Constantine, Sarah McCann, Max Ritvo,
Angelos Sakkis, Josephine Simple, Brian Sneeden, & Karen Van Dyck

Jerzy Ficowski | *Everything I Don't Know*
tr. Jennifer Grotz & Piotr Sommer
PEN AWARD FOR POETRY IN TRANSLATION

Antonio Gamoneda | *Book of the Cold*
tr. Katherine M. Hedeen & Víctor Rodríguez Núñez

Maria Laina | *Hers*
tr. Karen Van Dyck

Maria Laina | *Rose Fear*
tr. Sarah McCann

Perrin Langda | *A Few Microseconds on Earth*
tr. Pauline Levy Valensi

Elisabeth Rynell | *Night Talks*
tr. Rika Lesser

Giovanni Pascoli | *Last Dream*
tr. Geoffrey Brock
RAIZISS/DE PALCHI TRANSLATION AWARD

Rainer Maria Rilke | *Where the Paths Do Not Go*
tr. Burton Pike

Ardengo Soffici | *Simultaneities & Lyric Chemisms*
tr. Olivia E. Sears

Ye Lijun | *My Mountain Country*
tr. Fiona Sze-Lorrain

Verónica Zondek | *Cold Fire*
tr. Katherine Silver